# Thimble Flood

By Gary Dembs

ISBN: 978-1-4834-3665-4 (sc)
ISBN: 978-1-4834-3664-7 (e)

Lulu Publishing Services rev. date: 09/22/2015

**Thimble Flood**
**Dedications To:**
My lovely and supportive wife, Jan
My original writing muse in Houston – Jim Hendrick (Bird The Good)
My Southfield High School Creative Writing Teacher – Joan Cowell
Jason Grube for Cover Photography

# CONTENTS

# CHAPTER

# 1

# WELCOME TO THE DISTILLERY

# ANYTHING FOR FELLOWSHIP

"Best of Paris"
His verse was voted
At the Harrisburg fair,
Where legions of fireflies
Illuminated Hemingway
Much to his chagrin

2 more glasses of interference
And he'll kiss her,
Or worse,
Drag her to
The Moroccan donkey festival --

Anything for fellowship

Staring across her backyard
Watching her change skirts
In the window frame

(May 31, 2011)

# SADNESS AND RAZOR BLADES

Despair isn't relative, it's here,
Locked inside this darkened bathroom,
Sadness and razor blades, wondering
Which cut counts?

And, of course, they'll remember him,
Frozen to the bar stool in blood,
To be washed away later
By the children of the beggars of
Peace, yet he remains
Soiled in solitude, build-up and
Release

Every cluttered remake
Every man, an excuse,
Am I the only one hundred-percenter
Anxious for truth?

Why can't my level be reached?

When a promise can't be delivered, just sent
Then finally acted upon without regret,
Will my mold then be perfection?

This knowledge of impossibilities keeps me mingled,

The day is here, but

The way is blighted by ice and disease

And I need you now,

At least generically, to understand.

(January, 1995)

# BRIEFEST OF BRIEF MOMENTS

Adam,
Oh
Adam,

They buried you a month ago today
into the still soil of a Mt. Clemens cemetery
When, instead, you should have been
Here, playing

I miss you
And want you
To know
I really didn't want you
To go
So soon

We had the briefest
Of brief moments together,
You and mom and I, and
That short time,
Compared to the life we had planned
Together,
Makes me cry, uncontrollably

Why did you have to die?

Now you are alone,
Unable to hug
And we
Are unable to hug you back

So let the only hug we had
Sustain you, dear Adam,
Know our love contained you
And know
We will never forget
You

(April,1990)

# CAYENNE PEPPER BREAKFAST

Take the hari-kari pen,
Then make an incision
Above the navel,
Through the colon,
Until my stool bleeds into it,
And only hope to feel better later
If I can feel, at all

Call 911!
Call G-D!
Call Mom!

I'm not really in touch with reality,
Just enough to splinter
And earn a living,
But tonight I'm off the grid,

Rage ego, masculinity
Tug at the parachute straps
Until I can sleep, and
Even if it comes
I won't be able to stop it

Because in the morning
It is cayenne pepper
For breakfast, again

Therapy only distends
And I'll wet my pants
Before the caked shit is dry


(July, 1994)

# WHY WRITE?

Why write of SUICIDE?

Just to tease the psychologist?

(December 18, 1997)

# DRAGGING BACK THE ACCIDENT

Clear the glass shards
From the cellophane
With just your lower teeth

Step over your dead baby's body
And trip on the swollen fetal sac
Cracking your vertebrae

Plug her vagina with a doctor's fist
And swallow the cacophony of toxemia

Sob in the nursing home parking lot,
Where every brick sponges and suppresses
Memories holocaustal
For the cruise-goers
From Minsk

Watch my mother-in-law fade daily
Distracting our pregnancy procedures

The death of hope of death of hope
Of months, upon months of
Feeling like pus

(July 20, 1997)

# DANTE'S CAVE-INS

Time to clean the ceiling, for

The dungeon floor's already pristine

Yosemite's a geyser, yes,

But no sir,

Dante's cave-ins

Haven't gotten to me

(Yet)

# FEARING ALABASTER

Lower than a toothpick in urine

Nothing but stucco and mirrors

Fearing alabaster

Or blackened piano keys

Shaking

For

Spring

To catapult depression

Forward

Back into my intestines, feeling

Lower than a toothpick

In urine

(March 17, 1996)

# FLAYED & FLAWED (TUESDAY)

Affirming nothing except real time intellectual atrophy

He

Stabbed his shadow repeatedly

Killing

His                                                            anti-climatic self

In a coffee shop grenade explosion

A Grande caffieneated

Suicide, slicing sorrow

To                                                            embrace sky and

Sensibility

On a

        flayed & flawed

              (Tuesday)

                      (January 24, 2012)

# FREE UNTIL MY TASTE BUDS BLED

I snatched the scissors,
Opened            them
And sliced my tongue
D
O
W
N
W
A
R
D


Trying to manage the moment
Until my taste buds bled

Conflict, raised voices
Chaos and perceived

                              abandonment

Why won't she be coming back                    home?

And, so I live
In the common wealth of pain
With this badge of discouragement
And a depressive, shrinking brain


                                        (March 10/13, 1997)

# VENOM SEEMS APPROPRIATE

Keep telling me everything's fine!

You bitch,
I'll rip your eyes out so that you'll never have to see
Me again

I'll tell you how I feel –
I feel fine because i haven't had your guilt and manipulation
Shoveddownmythroat for months

Merry Christmas, my ass!!
You're the Virgin Mary, unmarried,
A lost soul waiting for Jesus, or
Your son, your brother, your father,
The man you can never have
Because I am gone

Leave me alone.
Stay away.
You are only a horse-shit memory
And that's the way I want it to
Stay

I could smack you….telling me everything is fine….it wasn't fine
I never shared my juices with you. It wasn't fine. You weren't mine…
You were never even your own. Deal with your schizophrenia on your time.

I'm not listening anymore!
Venom, seems appropriate.

# HELD IN ABEYANCE BY ANGELS

On my way from the gravesite
I carried the watering can at an

        A
          N
            G
              L
                E

So that the last drops evaporated in the sun
Before they hit the cement,
Held in abeyance by

                S
              L
            E
          G
        N
      A

To reappear on my cheek
At a later moment of
A
N
G
U
I
S
H
,
 
,
 
,
 
,

(June, 1991)

# HURT, YET LOVED (ORPHAN)

An orphan, now

Blind, but watchful

Hurt,

Yet loved

By my father

And mother

May 16, 2013 (DAD)

# LIMBLESS LEGEND (COPENHAGEN)

(I'm the)
Limbless legend
Whose stories fill
Rockless quarries

Where I become
Flummoxed by
Flawless synonyms
Others utter

I stray shyly away
From encroaching screens,
Here on the Metroplex
Of pink pumps
And yellowed dreams

Copenhagen, it seems,
Would be a good spot for vacationing, about now
Where uneven billy-goats eat gelatin
Off the cigar factory floors

Yet, here I stay in the frozen kinesiology of the forgiven
Where, somewhere,
My progeny flourishes
On someone else's sleeve
Oh, how I wanted to plant
Oh, how I've not,
Nourishing nothing

He or she is probably
Wasting vast hours
Sitting under a catalpa tree
Reading, trying hard to forget
Childhood hymns,
And create, instead
Allegories

(August 14, 2012)

# RED LIGHT THAT NEVER APPEARS ON THE FREEWAY

Subversive enemy,
Pi squared, unknown
The eye is drawn immediately to the light, yet
The pupil dilates, as her
Eyelashes tiptoe down the broken white lines
Stopping every fifteen feet
For the red light that never appears on the freeway

I can see in the dark, even without headlights
Through the reflective tape over your eyes,
Asleep at the wheel of fortune, I am

Pugnacious flirt,
Licks her lips across my brain, again,
Then closes my eyes with her toes, so
That her fingers can't get in the way of feeling
Anything but tomorrow

Why is heat white, and
Black darkness cold?
Why not just save yourself for Tuesday, when the snow falls,
Black snow which never melts, yet still
Forms handshakes in the tar.

Decadence can never be borderline, and
Sweat forms only below the surface, until it is shared,
Wiped by the inhuman wind, and they say
Gentlemen prefer blondes, but it's because the eye focuses on parted hair,

In the sun, and oftentimes
The moon glows at sunrise, and
The empty chair refrain is still
Solemnity

There is a drawer somewhere that has been opened 1000 times, but never by the same
Fingertips,
An endless drawer, in an antique desk, where the inkwell overflowed, often,
And the spill
Became an amorphous shadow, but in it, I can just make out
An animated face, once I've emptied the champagne carafe

And she rises, as if to inquire, but thinks twice, blinks, then is escorted, but not by me
Out of the restaurant, killed in traffic, in less than two minutes,
It's on videotape, for posterity, for the glory of the evening news, and
I stumble into obscurity, until sunrise,
When the dead reawake

Oh, the excused behavior of the artist
Instant pen photography, a future memory
Where the kids are fine and the wife is o.k.
Yet i still live inside this
Helium                                              N
                                               O
                                      O
                          L
                    L
              A
B

Scratching elastic plastic to get out and slip down the

S
T
R
I
N
G
To walk along the telephone wires, listening
To other people talk about themselves, and
Not about me.

Never satiated on a binge

Expulsion is ever-present, even
In public places, and
The only embarrassment comes from others' pity
But I'm satisfied to go
On.

Bartender, another scotch, please.

(August, 1984)

# GINSBERG ANN ARBOR

Aren't we all caricatures,
Plaintive and seducing
Wading through Billie Holliday's
Smoke and desire through
Frank Sinatra's
American jazz era, with
Thoughts of
Every form of freedom
As suppression tries to mirror us
Into a new eon,
February between commemorations
And some sign of spring
Amidst Greek texts
In the Shaman Drug bookstore,
Ann Arbor,
Standing next to a ladder
For extensions of mind
Of being tall
And unbound

And, if he breathes in
He can remember Tangiers,
Dirges, funeral pyres, and
Still sense the crowd's
Anticipation,
Nervous
Smiles
All around

(February, 1994)

# EMPTY PARK BENCH & STADIUMS

My mind is an empty place right now, filled
With lonely park benches, snowy streets,
4 a.m.

I wander through that emptiness
Until I strike a solid
Chord, which itself is
Loneliness,
Which is also a
Temporary state

For, my mind is a fertile place,
Right now,
Images of carnivals, stadiums,
Involvement, touching, wonderment
Of what it was like
When my mind was an empty place

Right now

(May, 1982)

# DODGE BALL

It's all about Debbie Stotsky and dodgeball. She died, maybe in 3rd grade, some kidney thing, her cheeks were always so rosy. But Mr. Bojanszyk, our gym teacher at Schoenhals Elementary School, survived, before he retired from the same job, well into his sixties, just a few years ago. Who remembers these people, except me and maybe Jeff Pont?

Who can conjure the intricacies of the multi-purpose room, used as our gym, our lunchroom our assembly room, that provided a Formica forum to discuss last night's episode of Batman or the Monkees, with Levin and Seltzer, or how the cafeteria trays matched the color of our safety boy belts, handed out in the hierarchy of inclusion, and who would not want to be a safety boy anyway, it did come with a badge you know.

The same room where as a Cub Scout, no make that a Webelo, I came in last in the Pinewood Derby, no trip to Akron, for this guy, I wasn't used to using sandpaper, and I needed, even back then, to slow it down a notch, and at 8 years old, I wanted to be part of the cool group, that even Applebaum and Kurtz were part of.

It was a revelation to learn that Mrs. Lieberman, could be both the lunch-room lady and my brother Howard's friend Wally's mother (no relation to The Beaver), even though Wally did grow up to be a large animal veterinarian, in Washington State (he never even owned a horse), or Jeff Sharkey, no one called him Jeffery, the seeds of accountancy, had not yet been planted, or so it would seem, in blighted reflection.

I met Gordie Howe in that room, waiting in line for him to sign a postcard, of which I still have up in my office, Gordie Fucking Howe! somewhere around 1971-72, when I was a bit older and the multi-purpose room still seemed so big, as big as Howe's shoulders. It's the reverence that we had for adults, whether gym teachers or hockey stars, who could never recall our names, but we knew theirs, even now. As Gordie lays dying in Texas, I doubt he thinks of me. But my teachers, shit, I can remember all their names, 2nd grade through 6th, and I wonder if they're dead or in their 80's by now, Samuelson, half of second grade, my having come over from Birney, 1964; Mrs. Castle, 3rd; Mrs. West, 4th; Mrs. Droz, 5th, I head she had MS; and Mrs. Granitz, 6th, I didn't have Mrs. Munns (then Nemzick,) didn't know teachers got married. I even remember the names of the teachers I didn't have; Mrs. Cole, Mr. Banks…

And the dodge ball games, taken outside against the back wall of the school in the spring of 1965, targeting Nancy Miller in particular, because she was so weird and her frizzy hair was easy to hit with the ball, remembering the indoor gym again, playing "Bringing Home the Bacon", stealing a bowling pin from the middle of the floor before being pelted, with the ubiquitous dodge ball, and that was weird because as Jewish boys, it was the only bacon we could touch!

Supposedly, Randi Lansky became a born-again, what the hell happened in that household, or any of ours, for that matter. Poor Alan Schon, died in second grade, hit by a car coming home from Mark Rosenbaum's house, across Southfield Road. Who thinks of him, or if Arna Wexler survived? And if you think this is all meaningless, it isn't because

Some of us dodge, some dart, some died, some didn't give a shit, but I did and do.

I want to be written about or discovered in Carol Bensman's diary, from 1965. I want to be in Sonia Beck's will (just for sentimental reasons, no real money there).

He was a "nice" guy they said, even Lois Silverman, thought so, and generations onward, isn't that how most of us want to be remembered?

(November 19, 2014)

# FEAR....IN ALL ITS DEFINITIONS

Remember when you were five
And your mother dragged you out of the path of a car
Careening,
At 60 MPH?

Instant fear....right?

Your heart pounded faster than a construction worker ramming nails into a 2x4
Trying to put up one wall on a new house before lunch,
Anxious to finish, so that he wouldn't be fired.

(I am so scared.....)

Wise men shy away from predicting the future for fear that they may be right
And then where would I be?

(Control yourself.....)

The factory worker blocks an impending layoff out of his mind, right
Until the moment a notice is posted on the bulletin board,
(Slapped with uncertainty), next in line to pick up his final paycheck

Do you remember when we went out for dinner at Ouisi's Table in Houston
And forgot the credit card?
How we were so worried that the waiter wouldn't understand
And we would have to wash the dishes to pay for the meals.

(Stay cool. It's only a minor snag.)

My wife died last weekend
And I was so unsure I could go on living
But I did.

She didn't.
But she has nothing to fear anymore.

I do.

Where am I going to find the cash to pay the mortgage?
Payday isn't until next Friday and I have to pay for school supplies.

Right in the middle of my shower last Tuesday, I ran out of soap.
I'll never be clean by 8:30. No hope. What will my boss think?

Last night I partied until 2 a.m. What will I do?
I have an exam at 8 a.m.
This could be the difference between a "B" or a "C" in Oceanography
And I need a passing science grade if I'm going to make it into medical school.

My pants have a noticeable mustard stain on them.
Should I go home and change….run the risk of being late,
Or hide the stain with my hand…and later a napkin?

My smoke alarm went off last night, and I was frightened.
I was so concerned. I was only cooking in my mind
And my ideas got too hot for my environment.
I was scared that I wouldn't be able to explain to the fireman just how it happened.

(It's only me.
Will I ever be sure of anything?
Or is that what makes life so intriguing?)

A young couple sits in the corner of a secluded restaurant, together but alone.
Only married a week when they find they can't handle life together any more.
But who is keeping score?

(Where will I go from here?)

The artist struggles with the fear of acceptance,
Knowing that to please others, he must be true to himself
And he is worried.

What will they think?

When I was seven, I was upset. I was chosen last on the kickball team, 3 weeks in a row,
And I felt unwanted. Now,
I own the N.Y. Mets and I'm not sure if we can win the pennant this year.

I sweep the streets of Newark. How much lower can you go?
But, I love my job.
I found a $50.00 bill on the ground last night, and I wasn't sure if i should keep it.
If I do, I don't want to get caught. What would my kids think?

I went out on a date on Saturday and ordered a dinner that ran $30.00.
Should I have opted only for an appetizer? I am on a diet and I'll never attract the
perfect woman if I don't lose 25 pounds by Thanksgiving.

(What will I do?)
What will she think?

Damn, I really wanted to watch that documentary on crime last night.
But my TV was stolen,
My kids were kidnapped,

And my secretary shot herself on her lunch hour.
Now those contracts will never get to Dallas on time.

But why go through life unaffected?

I'm not sure if I can stand the pressure of matching my clothes in the morning.
I get ulcers waiting for the final score of the Ram's game on Sundays,
But could care less if my wife is sleeping with the gardener.
I crashed my car into a boulder last Friday.
I was worried that I couldn't get it up on the weekend, but I had no trouble
When I wanted to fantasize, alone, on a Wednesday.

(What will G-D think?)

Maybe I care too much....
Chessboard options on a checkerboard when the game is over and
all my friends have gone home.

(I am alone. Shaking,
But trying not to be afraid.)

I used to worry about getting my allowance, so I could buy candy, and then had
thoughts of stealing from the drugstore...
Now, I want to go home to sleep
And not be concerned that the sun would rise
And so would I.

It's only Thursday.
Wait until the weekend.

(1984)

# CHAPTER

# INTO A BLENDER

# ALWAYS MOVING FROM SOMETHING I HAVEN'T EVEN STARTED

A second ago I was angry,
Yet I don't remember what for

Earlier today, I was joyful,
But I don't believe it

And, as my poetry gets colder
Than my frozen fingers,
Lines linger

Now, I have that vulnerable freeway feeling, again

Always moving from something
I haven't even started

(December 26, 2014)

# A SUNDAY GROWING UP

The Free Press,
Always
The Detroit Free Press,
Sunday's before going to
Grandpa and Grandma Ribiat's,
Off Dexter, near Davison,
First house north of the
Grocery store (later to be gutted in the riots)
With its Romanesque gutters and
Downstairs rented flat,
Bouncing marbles
Into my brother Howard's
Shirt pocket
From the second floor porch
Upstairs, a
Sepia toned spiral lamp
Next to their grandson Larry's
High school graduation picture,
Which hung over you like the smell
of noodle soup, and
Remembering my first look at a rotary phone,
Tuller exchange

(March, 1993)

# ALL VANITY CEASED

Four doctors were sitting around the break room table
Pushing opinions like prescriptions

And the middle –aged physician, who
Practiced middle-ages medicine spoke first

"Hair loss is the scourge of human-kind!"

And before those words could reach the others' ears
he realized that he was almost entirely bald

"Wrinkles!" Stated another
"yes, wrinkles," said a third

"Men who grow old gracefully, were never graceful, when they were young,"
said yet another

Just then the head nurse walked in and announced that
their hospital would start performing abortions
and it was at that moment
all vanity ceased

(January, 1987)

# APPARITIONS (I)

Orphans, now

And sometimes apparitions,

Our life force is gone,

Yet we remain spawn,

Bro's broken,

Our father's done

(May, 2013)

# ASHTRAY'S NOT CLEAR

Deep inside the metal cellophane siphons of digestion
Lies the pumice-tile afterglow of a Bailey's Irish Crème
Mirroring L.A., while somewhere near Latrobe, PA the
Left earlobe on Arnold Palmer freezes in a sand trap,
Elsewhere, Bridget Bardot blows her nose into minks
And into the sleeves of thieves, stealing her glances,
While a Marcello Mastrioanni fan grieves over a dead
Dream image of one Cary Grant, & it's hard to believe
Glass for dessert and the ashtray's not yet clear and,
We linger, smoky smiles and – Grand Canyon teeth –

(December 20, 1996)

# ATLANTA CONSTITUTION

Ah....southern simplicity

Sitting in the mild chill,

Sippin' scotch,

Shooing away the cat

Friday afternoon

After the Constitution

Is read

And as the nihilistic rocker sounds

D

I

S

S

I

P

A

T

E

Over the convenience store hills

I settle

Into quiet complacency

And await

                                    nothing

(December,1985)

# BRITTLE CRUST

Thick as

Tusk or

Marrow

Yet brittle

As crust

And as

Narrow

(September 24, 2012)

# BULLSHIT STANDARDS

I'd like to get my friends off the hook
For not living up to my standards,
But really,
What kind of bullshit is that?

(February 13, 2014)

# CAPITALCOMMUNISM

We sell Szechuan as Chinese food,
All in all, it never tastes very good

They sell Marlboros and Cadillacs,
We drive Buicks
They drive yaks
Oh, to live off each other's
Backs

It's Capitalcommunism
A flawless schism,
7 billion sold here
7 billion live there, but
Who cares?

No matter where your child is adopted or born
You open yourself up to nothing but scorn

We import egg rolls and too tall Yao Ming
They import rusted Oldsmobiles, and
Bonanza's reruns with too much Hop-Sing

Integrity is nowhere, practically speaking
Hell, they even went and renamed Peking

There is no continuity in taste or service
Tiananmen or Times Square, both make tourists nervous
Plastic is plastic
No matter its derivation

The world is increasingly
One red nation
The republican of Mao,
Under a similar dictatorship
(Now, not later, and ain't that a gyp)

(May 23-24, 2011)

# CHINESE JESUS GRAVITY

Gravity eyes dystopian
Chinese restaurant five
A.M., Yosemite does not
Stop burning overnight
And anti-semitism does not
Disappear when designer
Galliano is arrested or
When Jesus is resurrected, or when
Pop cola's culture's defined
By the side of an aluminum
Can and can
Jesus' role be portrayed effectively
In an undergarment commercial;
Depends -- what would Christ do?
Except be shrouded
In more mystery

(August 27, 2013)

# COUSINS (DEVOUT & DEVIANT)

Cousins, devout and deviant
One rabbinical, one
Mischievous,
Same DNA
Different upbringings,
Same sense of humor and of music
At least before 1973

Brilliance shown, by one
Through rigorous study
The other, manipulating
Through reckless "grooming"
And pornography

Oh, where did their lives go
After their shared time in the dorm
At the university?

One took to sickness,
One to Jerusalem
Now one in Netanya
One in a prison cell
Each praying
Into a different wall

How are we to understand?
How one can abuse children
And the other embrace them?
The dichotomy is inexplicable                    (September 18, 2013)

# CROSS ROAD REPENTENCE

If you're
Looking ahead to heaven,
Then
Why is your crucifix
Attached to
Your rear-view mirror?

(May 16, 2007)

# ECCENTRIC OBSERVER

Checkerboards & stripes
Are fall's clothing lines de jour --
I'll have the pan –seared tuna, with the
Swordfish menu hype and Dewars

Champagne & crumbs
A half-drunk coed in a bun,
Sneering, on crutches, she
Clutches her earrings then
Dumps them clumsily
Into her purse
Waiting to take a sip of tequila,
Seething, squinting at today's special--
Prime rib bougainvillea
She decides against that
And as if she couldn't be louder
Finally settles on the jalapeño
Corn chowder, waitress
Torn tights, bruised lipstick, smiles wanly
For a larger tip

As, this eccentric observer
Is left buck-toothed, handshaking colleagues
Into blind, blustering laughter and vague recognition
I can't even remember Livonia's zip code or who played which position
Left out of conversations, amidst
Too much derision

And, with no overriding temptation to stay

(nervous and lonely), I prey on the Zen of semi-colons

Splayed onto this page, and

Into the Bodhisattva of bad prose

I think I'll go home now

And

Blow my (nose)

(October 14, 1996)

# EVERYTHING IN PAIRS, EXCEPT ME & THE LORD

They say he didn't look good with a frown
And no one really understood
That compassion only kills itself
In sort of a greed-suicide
When the knife is handed over
After another round of solitaire is
Lost
Because kings
Don't lie
Over queens
And I'm tired of being jacked
Around
By missing persons

He was a brilliant writer,
When he wrote
A brilliant drinker, too

Tar & nicotine
Chivas & soda
Everything in pairs
Except me and the lord

(June 1985)

# FALSE ZUCKERBERG

Oh, you ruptured culture vultures…..

Bolstered only by Brahms and
Codeine, I go venturing into Highland Park,
A patina of foster homes, carpetless
With rocking chairs, paralyzed in place

"When you get the system down", i am told
"you can become tomorrow's Einstein"

Until then,
You must snake through the mosh pits
Or become
Just another false Zuckerberg,
Brainstorming worthless dreams

(April 2, 2011)

# FLEEING LEUKEMIA

Colored, glossy Mercedes'
Streaming out of Birmingham
Like white blood cells
Fleeing leukemia
Faster than a fly
Foreclosing on
Something which
Is not food

(June 12, 2000)

# LEAKY LOBSTER BOAT

Tired of telling
Uncle Bill Aunt
Greta passed away in
1998, over & over,
So
Again, we
Re-gift her life to him
So, he'll stop
Re-grieving,
Believing
Her submerged ship
Will resurface,
On the horizon line
Which is his dream-state, in
The calamity of calmness
That is Alzheimer's

And on the rhyming, yet choppy waves,
Of life's leaky lobster boat,
He rides out
On the ship he once captained
But now cannot steer.

(February 22, 2013)

# OLD MOTH

That old moth – memory
Separates the cloth
From The cloth
Ing

(January 29, 2013)

# PAP SMEAR SMIRK

Give up
That pap smear smirk and
Strapless frown

Survive

Then absolve today
In crushed smoke
And the aftertaste
Of a
Bitter
Birmingham morning

(June, 1995)

# PONTCHATRAIN RAIN

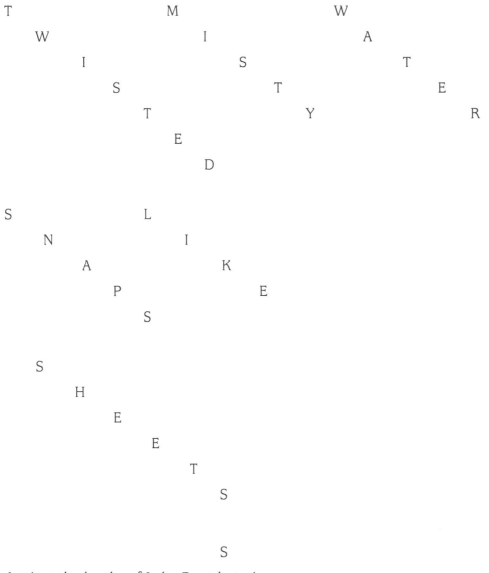

Against the banks of Lake Pontchatrain

Anesthetizes streets
And everything

Remains stationary
Except

      my

         mind

And the waves

      of my

       soul

Where there's no need

For shelter

(June,1983)

# QUANTIFYING NEW MEXICO

Here I am
Once again
Quantifying
New Mexico

(June 17, 1999)

# QUICK AS CANNONBALLS

Quick as cannonballs & muzzles are loaded, they're exploded,
Giving voice
To the voiceless
Once mute, expressionless
Conspiring elevators up

Struggling through
Internecine acupuncture
And whack-a-mole sleep deprivation
She wore sandpaper carbonation
Like prickly-pear earrings
Her cotton-blood bubbling
In the humidity

(March 21, 2012)

# ROBERTA, DIVERTED (TAXING CUSHIONS)

No providence, no
Karma, no shame,
No scheming, only
Freedom of choice,
Roberta, diverted

One thought to
Another, what to
Make for dinner on
Thursday that will
Honor her recently
Dead mother's recipes

No boldness for prose, or
Fiction, no discipline for
Quality journalism, either
Yet still as boisterous,
As a billiard ball on break,
Taxing cushions, and

What is loud to a flea
May not be to me, like
Biscuit to butter,
Rouge to cheek,
These Monday's
Are not for the

Meek                                      (March 17-18, 2014)

# SEX ME UP TO VENUS (FROM THE FOGGY BOTTOM RAIN)

I'm a Roman pagan
Feasting like its 14th Century Sicily
What a slob, throwing back sour mash
All's swell that ends swill

An incredible 30 hours, so far
Gone, no room for grumbling
Only for gratification, later

Bustling busboys, pleasing
A maitre d' minor
As Wolf Blitzer mimics Chopin
And Michael Bloomberg's butler
(on someone's dole)
Tosses twenties at the late
Judy Garland's aura
In the Foggy Bottom rain

And, (this is so weird)
Confederate whores,
I see, are puking again
Into General Lee's beard

Having a lovely
Bryon Gysin time,
Delving into
Schooner derivatives'
I need some gin
To sloe me down

I can't believe I'm here,
A frozen mediator, anxious
To dance

So sex me up to Venus,
Where I'll take my planetary chances

(November 7, 2013)

# SORBET FROM THE SORBONNE

So what

If she wants to go to culinary school

And get a Masters from the Sorbonne in sorbet,

Here with her English teacher father

Who's paying for her schooling, both

Offering only tight-lipped clichés

"You're my favorite dominant" she said

While slyly looking away,

Dad apologizes

And she demurs

For the sake of the check signer, it's deriguere

Both admitting nonchalance

After 20 years

18 methods behind gurgling and babble

Wanting not to be here

The prima donna

Digs into her asparagus,

And he into his beer,

Disengaged, yet both still

Displaying the familial acuity

Of the truly enraged

(January 22, 1996)

# SPECTACULAR YELLOW LOTTERY

Spectacular

Yellow lottery

Dandelion lawn sisters

They'll remember none of this

When they are 76

(Yet I will)

(April 18, 2012)

# SUBSTITUTING JAZZ FOR CLASS SEPARATION

Lactating clowns
Juggling tiramisu, I'm
Drinking decaf hazelnut
While frisking the espresso
For any sort of
Telegraphic integration

She has a distrustful smile
Bobbing, weaving
Through the coffee shop
All Nike logoed
Under a deflated Afro
Here after midnight mass.
Substituting jazz
For class separation
Thrown together in
Wide ties and pastel minks

And while I project, I pause
Because Allen Ginsberg might die soon
And I must pick up his pen
To mix inkblood
Into the camouflage of the Sun(day)

(December 1995)

# TEXAS NEXUS

Texas nexus
Jesus in a Lexus
Lotsa red-necked
Freckled Hyde's
And Jekyll's here
Gun-rack, six-pack
Slackers,
G.W. Bush
Backers
Proud,
Hell, even
Nolan Ryan
For crying'
Out loud

(August 2, 2011)

# VLADIMIR'S JAWBONE

My brother Vladimir's jawbone was barely visible in the ink
I used a magnifying glass to insure it was his.

I had just spoken to him, hours earlier

A 7 year old, in a Jakarta forest
Reacted in horror
Upon finding Vlad's still
Burning body

Experimental airplanes sometimes do vanish
Onto volcanoes
As do memories

Of tomorrow's dinner, scheduled
But will never have
Oh, but to have him back
I didn't want to share him this way;
Tomorrow's
New York Times' lead story
Grotesquely displayed

(May 11, 2012)

# VINTAGE FIRE

Possessions, once
Now memories, consumed
Vintage fire
In a second-hand room

Stuff,
Rebuffed,
Sold for cash
Now ash,
Fake lashes and
Faux fur,
Hatless mannequins
Wondering
Who set this blaze
And who is to blame,
Him or her?

In aisle two,
Liquefied Llardo figurines
Repaint a Norman Rockwell barbershop scene,
In this Saturday evening
Post toasty dream

An early 20<sup>th</sup> century globe
Drips Damascus onto Bridget Bardot,
Disrobing,
Yet the nearby bible just singes,
Stays open to Job,

And I curse myself, out in front
Over the Tony the Tiger cereal bowls i sold

Three five hundred
Caesars Palace poker chips
Burn to a crisp, as do
Bela Lugosi's gross, wax lips
Everything's disgusting
And caked with the oil
Of 400,000 fingerprints

Six melted metal thimbles
Flood
A Gimbel's catalog
And a set of 20's salt & pepper shakers,
Which used to be a cat and a dog

So let this conflagration be a lesson to the arsonist;
When careless with lit wicks,
Everything, including your memory,
Eventually sticks

# DEEP TRACKS GRAND RIVER

From my sandcastle wheelchair, electric
Pigeon-shit in my hair,
Graffitti'd streetwalkers
Jaywalking to Jericho
eight plastic bag indentations
On each arm,
Outside the basilica
Where filterless smoke rings
A Hindu temple fire
Escape

I see grave
Diggers in sun-dresses, laconic
Lamp-post leaners, post wet
Dreamers, no nearby dry cleaners
Homeless men, with
Burned fingers and bleeding
Ulcers,
Deep tracks
Grand River, Ave.

I see a silver, swerving
Schwinn, seatless,
Rider straddling duck-taped handlebars,
He stops, stalls into a wheelie, using
A Cadillac hubcap as his ego-mirror
And a Hires' Root Beer bottle-cap
As an eye-patch,

Which
Queers it all

Coming up on Fenkell,
Chugging, filterless Faygo
By the liter, life's
Cheaters, in wife
Beaters, rapping rhyme,
Contemplating hate
Crimes

# SEVEN SOWS

Under

My wholly-owned gate

Of sanity

Any

Misogyny

Is likely

Overneath

The

Underpass

Near the

Park

As the rabbi

Passes gas

And seven sows

Bleed to death

In Baghdad

(August 1, 1997)

# CHAPTER

3

# ACCUMULATED STEALTH

# CUBA LIPWARD

Lifting a Cuba Libra lipward
Martinez bends on U.S.soil,
Kissprints of Havana sugar
Canes split & sucked open -
Spitting into the Atlantic O &
Pissing off Castro - o yeah,
As Maria Olezabel wipes an
Ear with her sleeve, grandly
Her azure tan cheek, saltier
Than her memories, as tears,
Mingle, she's not upset, or oh
But pacific, walking on every,
Waterfall, and atop the burned
Coals, her liberty in limbo as E.
Hemingway drifts away to Mich.

# SETBACKS TO SANITY

Dead man sitting,
Bored and burned
At the fuselage, it
Threatens my dise
ngagement of all
Phones and faxes,
This wounded vet
No rings for rede
mption, it, seems,
I'm formless and
Sliding through
Solitary looking
Glassy with 8 pm
Upon me, bloody
Cheeks awaiting
A leaky fibula, &
A thin appetite -
For sleep confi-
gurations, of 40
Spiraling pubics,
Eddying into the
Abyss, oblivious,
Cancerous dreams
And the flushing -
Extracts hopeless-
Ness, feeling end-
Less nights in deep

Sorrow, no gains,
And only setbacks
To my brittle san-
I     T     Y.

(November 25, 1997)

# HOW IT 21ST CENTURIED

Here's how it 21st Centuried,
Lee H. Oswald was a patsy &,
Never fired a shot in Dallas
Crossfire, 5th floor not the
6th, second shooter off the
Grassy knoll fence post, by
The railroad tracks, sewer
Hole hides the fatal shot &
The hitmen at Elm's corner
All Corsicans, mob paid and
Flown to Italy out of fear,
And that, my dear,
Is how it 21st Centuried

(October 7, 1998)

# JACKIE OH!

Jackie, oh
How you made such a bitter memory soothe
By imprinting the world with your courage and
Composure,
A widow, in one day

Today, you snapped your shutter shut
With your delicate white glove,
All worldly banality, gone

I would have loved to have chatted you up in Central Park last Sunday
On the final weekend of your life
Wracked, wearing a wig,
Soaking up your stories
The way you're pretty pink dress
Soaked up the blood in Dallas, that fateful
November day

Thinking back,
I was aghast, that your pillbox hat stayed put
As you brushed your bangs away, smiling

Three bangs later...

| | |
|---|---|
| The president's head | in a cross fire |
| So unreal | so brave |
| Chasing | Camelot's brain |
| Onto the trunk | of the black Lincoln |

And, I so wanted to discover
Who you thought killed your husband
But will allow you to fade without explanation

We will all remember your first color White House TV tour
And you're marriage to that boor Aristotle,
How fascinated we were whenever we heard your whispery voice
And how the press endlessly debated your lifestyle choices

Yes, I would have loved to talk about the secrets you took underground
The most famous woman in the world, hounded, daily
Only seeing who you wanted to see,
But you were "our" celebrity and
We could not just let you be the ex-pat,
Edited from the Kennedy family

You intertwined two billion lives,
Clutching the tightest, unwritten memoirs in history
And you refused to be interviewed
Even after false assassins
Were pursued

And you were buried, yesterday in Arlington,
May 24th, 1994
Next to Patrick and your stillborn daughter and
The man who you and the world all adored
The pernicious paparazzi, perching as always
To see if you left any crumbs at their door

And, in the end, we thank you, for letting us
Take a collective view
Into the zenith of an era, which
Has disappeared
With your death

Go softly now,
I know you and jack
Have a lot to share

(May 25, 1994)

# THE RELEASE OF THE EMERALD RHAPSODY

The release of the emerald rhapsody
All grit and casino gutters of glory,
Talk of deadlines in today's anagram

Max Julian negros, eating scones in
Motor homes, a S.M.A.R.T. bus driver
Dangle the mangled pylon, then its
A pirouette up the aluminum step,
For a cigarette break and you know
A pipe bombing could happen here, a
Front page declaration from empty
Vending machines, in Jerusalem, too,
As the valet kicks at the sidewalk, in
Asphyxiated paranoia it is August and
Like a legless horse, grounded, to be
Transporting ourselves to morning
Discovering mafia hit men in a rental
Car that will never make Columbus -
Having rusted away, much like I am &

Below the monk's transom, above the -
International river, this giver holds a
Pen, it's his best friend, and I ask again,
Are the Windsor fish and chips soggier
To you, are you wondering if Margaret
Trudeau has a slip on right now, and if I
Can feel my ass, sitting below the tow
Truck and next to the Ren Cen towers –

Reminded of a failure of fate and streetlights
Which illuminate my sallowness
Eating Dinty Moore Beef Stew in a can &
I can see why I won't make partner, for
I will not wear a tie, and everything's
Mechanical, except radon, and it seems
Like a storm, each way I turn, yes it is a
Tempest, a sexpot untouchable, but lo,
This river rock is hardly on the corner
Franklin St. & St. Antoine, anxious, as I'm
Sprinting up the fire escape to be taken
By crows shitting on 2x4's, & missing me...

# NIXON'S FUNERAL, TONIGHT

King Richard, tonight
You are dutifully Hellbound,
storm clouds following you
Even in death,
As the cruel sky,
Which you helped blacken,
Awaits your sordid soul

We'll remember your shoulders
Weighted in paranoia, your
Drooping jowls of defeat, your
Double face, smug,
Hands raised in your ridiculous
Peace sign salute, on that
Joyous August day, in '74
You were a political whore,
Who forever soiled the presidency,
Leaving generations of enemies
Who salute you,
With a single, middle finger

You were the broken bridge
Between trust in our government
And indignity toward our leaders,
You were about power at all costs
Always without honor,
While twice you seized it,

Leaving blood in the sand in deceit
From Saigon to Miami Beach,
From Washington D.C., to San Clemente,

You are but a dead log in a raped, republican fireplace,
Leaving historians
To pick apart you're tapes
You're legacy --
A brooding, national shadow
Of war and political debasement
As we'll write whatever we want,
Without challenge, with no modicum
Of defacement

And, as the halogen Yorba Linda sun
Melts down my brain this evening,
Whittier's favorite son
Enters Air Force One, a last time
As American flags fly
In full mast defiance
Signaling a final good riddance,
To the noxious Dick Nixon
And with much relief,
We don't have you to kick around anymore,
So a final fuck you
To our commander in cheat

(April 27, 1994)

# ZAPRUDER'S SNUFF FILM

I'm sitting atop Dallas' infamous grassy knoll today;
This is sure some crass historical perspective I'm
Witnessing, 35 years on, with
Opinions as varied
As shotgun shells

Lechers, hawking to the hurly-burly
(most of whom were not even born yet)
Faux patriots allowing themselves to be seen at
Half mast,

And as American and Texas flags fly full staff
I'm aghast
At everyone's naiveté

Seniors, soldiers, here in Dallas,
Transfixed
Smoking outlawed Cuban cigars
As if they were still in their 20's
Watching Abraham Zapruder's snuff film being made
Lost now
Amidst the puttering of motor scooters
And Dictabelt echoes

This Yankee is only here
To commemorate this fallacy
Which gave us our collective
Future
Then sniper quick,

I'll return to Detroit
To preach ad nauseum
To the apathetic

Our sons will know the real truth
Just as these politician's knew they were targets
And I remain somber, yet hyper
Knowing it wasn't only Mark Lane
Who knew who the real assassins were,
It was me too

(November 22, 1998)

# EDIT? FORGET IT!

Mood?

Wry.

Waiting for my poetry
To dry.

Edit?

Forget
It!

(August 26, 2013 – Upon Reciting To
Poet Laureate Natasha Tretheway)

# CORPORATE CAT-A-COMB

Putrid cat barf has floated again
Over the tops of the shag carpets
Seething in silent vermin victory,
Capitalists have screwed us again
Pressed into mediocre molecules,
Poised in crushed human toxicity
Greenbacks wall-to-wall chasing
Each other through cubicles, and
Frothing in the e-mail, at already
Disagreed to recommendations, a
Comforting of pure insecurity for
This insecure loyalist who's resume
Styles Stalin, with tendencies to try
Not too touch, for only the piano is
Purity, as the philosophy of poetry a
Waits for Einstein's brain to melt for
It mimics Jeffrey Dahlmer's & each are
In need of a comb & camaraderie, now


(November 29, 1995)

# BERLIN DETROIT

Awoke In Berlin Detroit,

Gas Into graffiti

And what were once

Synagogues

Are now

Trash receptacles

In both cities

(March 25, 2014)

# LINCOLN INSPECTION

The grassy knoll bullet blasts past my shoulder,
And triggers an emotional blitzkrieg
Crystallizing everything mystifying
For generations,
Recreating an assassination, here
At the Henry Ford Museum,
Reaching in to touch
The many fingerprinted
Lincoln

Out of my way…
I'm off to Parkland Hospital
To take in the crime and its clues
History,
Ordered to stand down
Clint Hill, grasping at Jackie
Both splayed on history's trunk,
Transcendent,
And Dallas' finest,
Later washing brain matter off
Their badges

The firing lines seems clear, from here,
A crossfire, from this man's inspection
Penetrating angles, crosshairs evident
A nation stupitified,
In the gun metal glow of the moment

And I bet he's glad they left his privates alone,

His brain, to this day, remains missing,

(Historians would say they were the same)

While somewhere far from Arlington, near Alsace Lorraine,

A buried Degaulle sips blood red fresh onion soup,

And Castro's whiskers still spike in enmity

We are never too old to form theories

Damn it, there were hundreds of witnesses,

This is what we fight for,

Freedom's endless war of expression

But today, it's time for this propagandist

To drop his pen, and head off into Dearborn's snowy infinity,

Awaiting further vivisection

(December, 1994)